EXTREME SPORTS AND STUNTS™

EXTREME AERIAL SILKS

Xina M. Uhl

rosen publishing's rosen central®
New York

For my tiny dancer, Michaela Marie

Published in 2020 by The Rosen Publishing Group, Inc.
29 East 21st Street, New York, NY 10010

First Edition

Library of Congress Cataloging-in-Publication Data

Names: Uhl, Xina M., author.
Title: Extreme aerial silks / Xina M. Uhl.
Description: New York : Rosen Central, 2020 | Series: Extreme sports and stunts | Includes bibliographical references and index. | Audience: Grade 5 to 8.
Identifiers: LCCN 2019006449| ISBN 9781725347311 (library bound) | ISBN 9781725347304 (pbk.)
Subjects: LCSH: Aerialists—Juvenile literature. | Circus performers—Juvenile literature. | Circus—Juvenile literature.
Classification: LCC GV1817 .U45 2019 | DDC 791.3—dc23
LC record available at https://lccn.loc.gov/2019006449

Manufactured in the United States of America

Disclaimer: Do not attempt this sport without wearing proper safety gear and taking safety precautions.

CONTENTS

INTRODUCTION 4

CHAPTER ONE
FLYING THROUGH THE AIR WITH EASE 7

CHAPTER TWO
BENEFITS AND CHALLENGES OF BEING AN AERIALIST 17

CHAPTER THREE
TAKING THE NEXT STEP 25

CHAPTER FOUR
STARS OF THE SILKS 32

GLOSSARY 40
FOR MORE INFORMATION 41
FOR FURTHER READING 43
BIBLIOGRAPHY 44
INDEX 46

INTRODUCTION

A singer stands on a stage, illuminated by a dim light. He croons a wistful song as the audience listens intently. Behind him, long, red silks tow a female aerialist performer upward. She is wrapped from head to toe in the silks.

Suddenly, she flips upside down and does a split. Releasing her hold on the silks above her, she grabs the ends, which hang off her outstretched legs. She dangles in the air more than 12 feet (3.65 meters) above the stage, held in place only by the foot and leg wraps. The silks billow out around her like a beautiful red carpet that dances on its own. As the song's tempo speeds up, the aerialist spins in time to the music. Her amazing contortions continue until the song ends—and the audience erupts into cheers and applause.

This scene, from a performance of the acrobatic show by Cirque du Soleil in Montreal, Canada, gives you a taste of just how beautiful and mesmerizing aerial silks can be. Learning this challenging and rewarding skill has become a hot new craze sweeping across North America. But this sport is not one that you should try to teach yourself. The risk of getting hurt is too high. Don't worry, though. There are plenty of opportunities to learn in a safe environment. Performing aerial silks can be done as part of an individual performance at a gym, yoga studio, dance studio, or fair, or part of a larger

Cirque du Soleil aerialist Ginger Griep-Ruiz performs a piece called "Silk Tissue." Aerialists traditionally don't wear safety gear during performances, so they take other safety precautions to avoid injury.

production, such as the popular Cirque du Soleil. Certified instructors are offering classes at local studios, camps, and circus arts schools.

Aerialists find many benefits from practicing with silks, everything from core and upper body strength, balance, and grace to discipline and self-assurance. The workout is intense, yet instructors stress that anyone can do it. While many girls and women perform with aerial silks, there are plenty of boys and men who are hooked on the sport, too.

This resource will highlight what aerial silks are, what equipment, training, and qualities one needs to perform them, and where and how to learn them safely. Extreme athletes will divulge their secrets for performing this exacting and beautiful sport.

CHAPTER ONE

FLYING THROUGH THE AIR WITH EASE

Aerial silks go by several names, including aerial tissue, aerial ribbons, and aerial curtains. Each refers to the same kind of performance: talented acrobats who make use of long, see-through silks anchored to the ceiling, allowing the aerialists to climb, twirl, drop, spin, and swing high above the ground. One of the newest forms of circus performances, it is also one of the most impressive since it provides viewers with a graceful, dazzling display of movement, color, and skill.

Though this aerialist is performing a difficult pose, she makes it look easy and graceful.

As the sport grows more popular, many people have become curious about it. Where did it come from? How does it work? And the most daring question of all: where can I learn how to do it?

ANCIENT ACTS OF DERRING-DO

No one knows who invented the first circus acts, but they probably came about early in human history. This form of entertainment involved performers folding their bodies into incredible positions, balancing one on top of another, flying through the air, and doing other fantastic feats. The ancient Romans coined the term "circus." To them, a circus was a large open-air arena where chariots raced, gladiators fought one another, and wrestling competitions took place.

With the fall of the Roman Empire came a long period when circuses fell out of favor. Then, in the late eighteenth century, Philip Astley created shows in which horses performed in large rings in front of crowds in London. Over time, Astley added other elements to his shows, including ropewalkers, tumblers, clowns, acrobats, and music. Astley's circus spread to France, and, in time, similar circuses popped up throughout Europe, and in the United States, Mexico, and Canada.

During the first half of the nineteenth century, many small circuses in the United States sprang up and traveled from place to place in a line of wagons. They featured clowns and performing animals like horses, elephants, and later, lions and tigers. Performers—sometimes from one family—often rode bareback on horses and leapt from animal to animal, balanced on top of trotting horses, and did other impressive acts. High-wire acts (or tightrope walkers) featured people who would walk across a thin wire suspended high above

Mexican aerialist Iram Ramirez contorts his body during a performance at the 2nd Annual US Aerial Championships in New York.

the ground without falling. Trapeze acts used swings to fly from place to place high in the air.

In the late nineteenth century, two partners, P. T. Barnum and James Anthony Bailey, started a popular circus called Barnum & Bailey's Greatest Show on Earth. The Ringling Brothers ran another well-known circus. Eventually, Barnum & Bailey joined forces with the Ringling Brothers to create a long-running show called Ringling Bros. and Barnum & Bailey Circus. The heyday of the circus ran from about 1880 through about 1920. Eventually, the popularity of the traditional circuses waned due to competing interests, such as sports, movies, and television. The Ringling Bros. and Barnum & Bailey Circus went out of business in 2017.

A NEW KIND OF CIRCUS

In the twentieth century, shows like the Ringling Bros. and Barnum & Bailey Circus were still operating, but other performers were creating new art forms inspired by the circus. In the 1970s, a trapeze artist named Terry Sendgraff created and taught what she called aerial dance in San Francisco. Aerial dance grew popular throughout the 1970s. This sport involves dance moves performed while the aerialist, wearing a harness, is suspended in the air from a cable or rope. Some forms of aerial dance involve the aerialist pushing off the floor or wall as part of the routine.

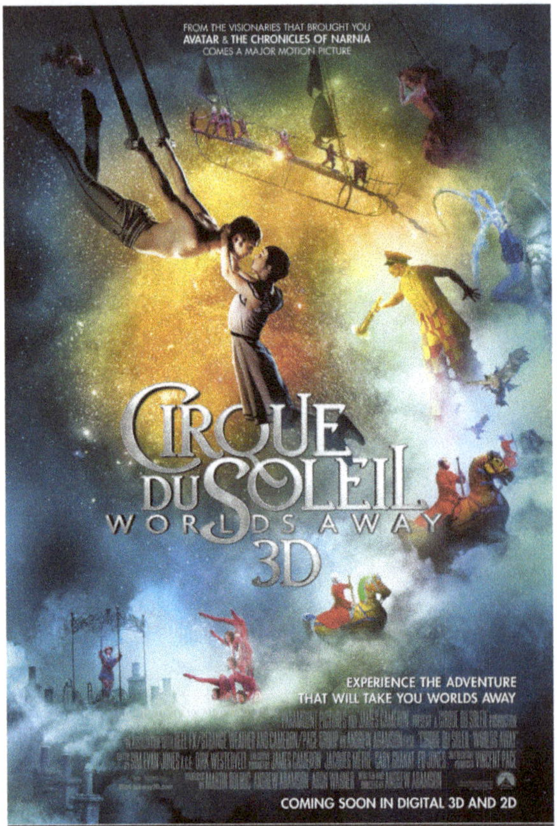

This poster advertises the film *Cirque du Soleil: Worlds Away*, about a young woman fascinated by an aerialist. The two travel through a dreamlike world together.

In 1984 in Montreal, Canada, a different kind of circus debuted—one that used only human acts—Cirque du Soleil. Cirque du Soleil reinvented the circus through their use of elaborate sets, high-tech light and music designs, and themed performances that used acrobats and aerial dancers to mesmerize audiences with daring jumps, leaps, somersaults, and more. While the origin of aerial silks can be traced to a French circus around 1959, Cirque du Soleil was the circus that brought aerial silks to the world's attention.

When Cirque du Soleil debuted in Los Angeles and Las Vegas, their shows quickly attracted renown. Over the years, they created different shows, such as *O*, *Kà*, *Ovo*, *Amalũna*,

FINDING LIVE PERFORMANCES

Perhaps you've seen aerialists perform with silks on YouTube videos or special television performances. While these may be impressive, they are nothing like seeing these performances live as part of an audience.

But where can you find them? The most obvious choice is to get tickets to one of Cirque du Soleil or Cirque de la Symphonie's shows. But these can be expensive. Such shows may not always be available in your area either. Smaller troupes, like Troupe Vertigo, may supply performers to ballets like *Swan Lake* or Pops shows that feature Broadway music hits. Again, tickets usually are pricey.

Aerial silks performers can appear at state and county fairs, local festivals, exhibitions by circus schools, and fitness studios, too. Keep your eyes peeled and you may find aerial silks performances in unlikely places, too. In 2016, students and instructors at Brigham Young University looked for a way to suspend an actor from a spider's web for their production of *Charlotte's Web*. The ability of aerial silks to allow a performer to spin and weave like a spider was the answer to their problem. The visual of actor Meagan Flinders spinning a web in the air helped transform her into a spider in the audience's minds.

and others, for more than 180 million spectators. Productions occurred in hundreds of cities in sixty countries.

Today, smaller circus troupes also exist. One is Cirque de la Symphonie. This circus company works with symphony orchestras worldwide. Their shows combine acrobats, aerialists, illusionists, contortionists, and jugglers with live classical music to create a visual and musical extravaganza.

THE INS AND OUTS OF A PERFORMANCE

Aerialists must learn certain moves and techniques when performing with silks. Such motions would be impossible without specialized equipment and fabrics, though. It's too bad that humans don't come equipped with the adaptations that allow birds to fly: feathers, wings, and hollow, light bones. Instead, we must rely on a complicated array of supports and fabrics to allow us to soar through the air.

The most important item of all is the silks themselves. This fabric is not actually made from silk, despite its name. Instead, it is made from denier polyester tricot. Tricot fabrics are often used for swimsuits and sportswear. The

This dancer holds onto an aerial silk. Despite its name, aerial silks are made from polyester or nylon instead of silk.

denier polyester tricot blend is designed to stretch very little from use. Nylon is also frequently used for aerial silks. A silk can either consist of one long piece of fabric or two pieces of fabric sewed together at the top. Next, silks aerialists usually apply rosin or hairspray to their palms to help them grip the silks without slipping.

Aerialists support their poses by tightly wrapping the fabric around their wrists, hands, feet, and ankles. This way, the aerialists are safe to perform a variety of movements.

Aerialists make use of a number of different apparatuses, or special items, to allow them to be suspended in midair. They include hanging ropes (also called *corde lisse*), straps, loops, hammocks, and slings. Hoops can be used as well. Also called lyra, this circular piece of equipment resembles a large metal hula hoop suspended in the air. Aerialists use the hoop to perform a number of poses—alone or with a partner—that involve spins, swings, and being raised and lowered from the ground. A trapeze, or a metal bar hanging from two ropes at either end (like a playground swing), is often placed high above the earth. Performers use it to stand still, swing, or fly from one trapeze to another (or to be caught by a fellow aerialist). Mats on the ground are a necessity to soften the blow in case the aerialists fall.

The rigging is an essential part of the equipment. Certified rigging professionals make use of steel or wooden beams as A-frames. Beams, scaffolds, and ladder bars can be placed on the rigging depending on the desired look and function. Hooks, clamps, and rings are placed at rig points that must be able to withstand about 1.1 tons (1 metric ton) of capacity load, though some professionals insist upon rigs that will handle about twice that capacity load. In other words, the forces created when aerialists swing, hang, and make other motions exert a lot of stress on the rigging. Because of that, it is essential that the rigging be designed to handle this amount of weight. It is essential for rigs to be regularly inspected for damage and maintained in order to be in the best working order possible. After all, lives depend on it!

In order for aerialists to perform on their rigging, they must first stretch with certain conditioning exercises. These exercises should be supervised by professional instructors. Next, the aerialists will wrap the silks under and around their feet to form a type of step to allow them to have a sturdy surface with which to climb up the silks. A sequence of carefully planned wraps, locks, drops, and other poses comes next. Each of these moves is possible only because of the performers' body strength and flexibility. Aerialists must practice for many hours to master the moves necessary for a routine. When they do so, they make the moves look easy, like a beautiful aerial dance.

CHAPTER TWO

BENEFITS AND CHALLENGES OF BEING AN AERIALIST

Certain words come up again and again when aerialists describe performing: “exciting,” “fun,” “thrilling,” “grace,” “control,” “confidence,” “strength,” and, of course, “workout.” Performers feed off the energy of the crowd. They are rewarded for their efforts by the audience’s applause and oohs-and-ahs. They also get the chance to dance and create a work of art with their movements.

Performers admit to being intimidated. After all, falling from heights is a real possibility. Even world-class aerialists, such as Christine Van Loo, feel that fear. In an interview with Ally Karsyn of the *Sioux City Journal*, Van Loo said, “I get scared. It’s just part of my job. I get scared and I do it anyway.”

Courage is a necessary part of performing moves such as flipping over, inverting, locking, and sliding. Unfortunately, injuries are bound to happen. Because of that, it is essential to learn how to fall correctly. By using the proper falling technique, performers can often avoid injury altogether.

An instructor helps to steady a beginning aerialist during a lesson. Having a skilled instructor is important when first starting out.

Though it may be part of their job to overcome fear, aerialists agree that even when it comes to beginners trying the sport, they recommend that you just go for it. Many say that anyone can learn to use aerial silks. While this may be true, given enough practice and instruction, it is necessary to have a skilled instructor to lead beginners through the ropes. While fun, aerial silks can also be dangerous and even fatal if not practiced correctly. Do not attempt to learn on your own. Opportunities to take classes, participate in camps, and join studios that train aerialists abound—and are becoming more numerous as the sport grows in popularity.

TRYING YOUR HAND AT SILKS PRACTICE

Beginners start out safely on the ground with poses that teach them how to handle the silks correctly and how to hold the proper positions and forms when moving. All aerialists start their routines with stretching. "Stretching is so important to help avoid injury and increase your range of motion through your joints and muscles," said aerialist Rony Elisara for the website Aerial Artistry®. "This will become increasingly valuable as you start to learn the trickier, more flexibility-based skills and advance through higher levels."

Stretches target the following areas of the body: upper, lower, and middle back, shoulders, hands, forearms, hamstrings, glutes, hip flexors, feet, and last, but not least, toes. Stretching takes place both before and after the aerial routine. Elisara also recommends stretching several times a week in addition to before and after the actual routine. This practice helps keep performers limber.

WHAT ABOUT OTHER TRAINING?

Many, but not all, aerialists come to the sport from disciplines ranging from dance and gymnastics to circus-specific practices like trapeze. Yoga and aerial yoga are also popular for those interested in the sport. While it is not strictly necessary to have experience with other forms of aerial sport, such activities can make a difference in your overall fitness.

Aerial silks instructors recommend a number of sports in addition to indoor aerials in order to help keep performers' bodies well balanced and to prevent injuries. Cardio training, such as jogging, swimming, walking, calisthenics, and high-intensity interval training (HIIT) is great preparation for aerial performance. Depending on what you enjoy and what challenges you, also consider Pilates, dance, hiking, yoga, cycling, and rock climbing.

While weight training can be good for you, it may not be as helpful to aerial performance as you would expect since the muscles you will be using are often different from those you engage as you train with weights. However, rope climbing, push-ups, leg raises (while hanging from a bar), and pull-ups/chin-ups are good strengthening exercises.

Yoga students finish their class with a brief meditation. Performing yoga can help aerialists with their own practice.

Instructors usually assume that new students have never tried aerial arts before and are not used to climbing, lifting, and pulling their own weight. Often, students start by resting in a length of fabric tied in a knot at the bottom (called a sling or hammock). This allows beginners to learn how the fabric feels and behaves before they trust it to support their body weight.

A CHALLENGE FOR BODY AND MIND

Christine Van Loo, a renowned aerialist, has performed with musicians including Paul McCartney, Britney Spears, and Aerosmith. Van Loo did not begin aerial silks training until she was twenty-seven years old, after many years of being a gymnast. In a video interview by the BBC, Van Loo talked about the learning process. "As an athlete and especially as an aerialist, I had to learn to get used to being uncomfortable. The first time I managed to climb all the way to the top of the rope, I was so exhausted that I slid down the rope like a fireman's pole. I looked at my hands. I had torn all the skin off my palms and fingers."

This painful injury nearly caused Van Loo to quit aerial silks before she even got started. Despite this, she continued to learn. In the BBC video interview, she said, "I had to give up being comfortable for a while. And I kept focusing on pulling my next climb up the rope, and no, it wasn't easy. It is painful climbing on shredded hands. It is scary climbing 30 feet [9.1m] on shredded hands." But, Van Loo cautioned, "The moment you quit in order to feel better is the moment your dream may die." As a frequent performer with Cirque de la Symphonie and a sought-after solo artist, Van Loo has accomplished her dream.

Next, most instructors teach students the techniques of wrapping the silks around their feet and how to hang from their arms. At first, most beginners are shaky and uncertain. Confidence and skill grow as students practice. So does strength. While upper-body strength is obviously important in this sport, core strength may be the most important of all. A strong core allows performers to use their bodies with deliberate care. In order to move with grace and purpose, performers must get to know every part of their bodies so that they can flow, twist, climb, and leap by using all of their strength.

The instructor makes sure beginners have basic moves down before they hang on silks at all (at first beginners stay close to the ground when practicing moves). It takes time and countless hours of practice before students are ready to rise as high as professional aerialists.

AN EXAMPLE ROUTINE

Certified aerial fitness instructor Kacey Cornell demonstrates a beginner's routine on her Instagram account. First, she takes hold of two strands of the silk, wraps her foot in a secure position, and arches her back. Next, she straightens her back and tilts her body so that she is leaning against one silk, with her feet separated. By extending both arms out straight, she demonstrates balance and core strength. Transitioning to a two-hand hold again, she arches her back and raises a knee, swinging gently back and forth.

Performances, whether by beginners or experts, do not usually last long, but stay in the range of five to eight minutes or fewer. Since acts are frequently choreographed around music, it must be selected carefully. Professionals who perform in circus acts such as Cirque du Soleil may stay in the air for ten to fifteen minutes a few times during the show.

Performers report that learning and practicing aerial silks challenges the body and the mind. At first, learners doubt they can find the strength and endurance to succeed. Little by little, they gain skills and soon enough, they find themselves climbing higher and higher. Succeeding in conquering such a challenging activity boosts confidence as well as strengthens performers' focus and concentration.

As with any skill, physical or mental, the key is practice. And

This performer demonstrates impressive balance and core strength as she performs a beautiful pose. Arm and shoulder strength are also crucial.

then more practice. While it is certainly possible to try silks every now and again, working with them regularly yields the best results.

Christine Van Loo explained part of her enjoyment of performing in Cirque de la Symphonie to reporter Ally Karsyn of the *Sioux City Journal*: "You don't just hear the music. You feel it coming up through your body. You become one of the instruments. It makes all the difference. It's the epitome of performing. Having an entire symphony orchestra beneath you, it doesn't get any better than that. I feel empowered when I'm up there. I feel very creative, inspired and, in turn, inspiring."

CHAPTER THREE

TAKING THE NEXT STEP

The practice of aerial silks brings many benefits. Confidence, strength, and the admiration of audiences are just some of them. But there are also risks. Some of the possible injuries can occur in any sport, such as bruises, sprains, broken limbs, and concussions. In addition to those, performers are at risk of pulled muscles, fabric burns, and overuse injuries of the back and shoulders. Serious injuries are more likely to happen when aerialists progress to the stage when they are performing 20 to 50 feet (6.1–15.2 m) above the ground with no safety harnesses or nets. Falls from those heights can even result in death. Lethal injuries, though rare among professional aerialists, do happen. If injuries strike even the most experienced aerialists, how can beginning aerialists stay safe and unharmed?

Aerial silks professionals make it look so easy. High in the air, they glide, swing, flip, and tumble, all while remaining safe. But the truth is that there are many precautions taken behind the scenes to make

The aerialist performing here demonstrates his confidence and strength as he twirls high above the floor. Both qualities make the performance beautiful despite the possibility of a fall or other injury.

sure the performers are safe. They start by doing lots and lots of rehearsals. Practicing their routine over and over again allows performers the opportunity to work out the kinks in the show. Rehearsals also cover what to do when things don't go as planned so that no one panics at the wrong moment.

Performers also rigorously test their equipment. Not only does equipment need to be in top working order, but it also needs to include fail-safe items to keep performers from hurting themselves. These can be emergency cut-off switches, skilled professionals watching the performers to make sure all is in order, and double- and triple-checking harnesses, rigging, and other equipment. Many circuses and acts employ registered professional engineers to review the acts for safety. The engineer uses a checklist to make sure all hardware and other equipment is in order.

Finally, everyone makes mistakes. By keeping that in mind, performers are taught to fall in the safest way.

LEARN FROM THE BEST

For beginners, the best insurance against injury while performing aerial silks is to find well-qualified instructors. Professionals have the education, experience, and knowledge to keep learners safe while encouraging them

Irish aerial silks instructor Jenny Higgins demonstrates for a group of her students in Gaza City, Gaza. Her maximum class size is eight people.

to take risks and have fun with aerial silks. Professional trainers know how to help you learn the complex wraps and positions to avoid injury, both immediate and long-term.

It is important to check the credentials of anyone who offers to teach aerial silks. Many circus arts training schools offer intensive training for instructors and performers alike. The New England Center for Circus Arts (NECCA) trains graduates for three years to become professional circus artists. Many graduates go on to perform with the likes of Cirque du Soliel, touring shows, festivals, on cruise ships, and other venues. The Circus Arts Institute in Atlanta offers an aerial teacher certification program that qualifies individuals to teach others. Also in Atlanta, the Sky Gym teacher certification program trains experts. As aerial arts become more popular across North America, it has become easier to find local gyms, studios, and independent instructors who are certified to teach all levels of students.

Trainers also offer aerial silks as therapy with new programs such as one offered by the Circus Arts Institute. In this program, students are taught to design routines for people to perform during traditional classes and during in-home sessions. Certification to use circus arts as therapy allows instructors to design routines that can be used to improve students' self-esteem, emotional control, and physical health.

By using "brain balancing" exercises, which strengthen both hemispheres of the brain, students' balance improves and their core muscles are strengthened. Students also learn to communicate, lead others, solve problems, develop empathy, and express themselves creatively. Another teacher training program helps instructors work with students who have special needs, learning challenges, and delays in coordination and other functions. These adaptive courses make it possible for people of almost all physical capabilities to learn aerial silks.

Have your parents make sure that the instructors have the appropriate education and certifications before you

NO LEGS? NO PROBLEM!

When Jen Bricker was born in Romania, her parents quickly placed her up for adoption. Why? Because she had been born without legs. Otherwise she was perfectly healthy, though. Her adoptive parents brought Jen to the United States, and she grew up in the Midwest. Despite her disability, Jen's adoptive parents never treated their daughter like she was unable to do what she wanted. They told her to take the word "can't" out of her vocabulary. By not doing everything for her, she had to figure out how to get what she wanted on her own.

Jen practiced gymnastics as a child and became so skilled that she competed against able-bodied gymnasts. As a result, she won many competitions, including a state title in high school.

In high school, Jen intended to go into the fashion industry. However, at nineteen years old, she moved to Orlando, Florida, where she worked for Disney World. From then on, she knew she wanted to perform instead. Her gymnastics experience led her to become an acrobat, and later, an aerialist. She has worked all over the world as an aerialist, from The Palazzo in Las Vegas to The ACT in Dubai, United Arab Emirates (UAE), and numerous shows in Australia. Today, she is also a motivational speaker. She has authored a best-selling memoir called *Everything Is Possible: Finding the Faith and Courage to Follow Your Dreams.*

choose one to teach you aerial silks. The American Circus Educators offer a safety program specifically designed to help programs and schools establish the safest possible practices based on a set of guidelines. Items in the guidelines include making sure that programs and schools have emergency plans in place, that equipment is kept in good working order and is inspected regularly, that class sizes are small, and that all instructors are certified in cardiopulmonary resuscitation (CPR) and first aid. Mats that absorb the impact of performers jumping and falling to the floor must be available. When choosing your instruction, it is a good idea for parents to ask about safety procedures and certifications at any class or studio you are thinking of attending.

UNDER THE BIG TOP

Those attracted to getting information and instruction from an official circus group can seek out the American Youth Circus Organization (AYCO). With a mission "to promote the participation of youth in circus arts and support circus educators," this association provides many opportunities to involve youth and educators in the wonderful world of circuses.

Around ten thousand kids, teenagers, and young adults under the age of twenty-six in the United States train and practice in the circus arts. These arts include not only aerial silks, but also acrobatics, trapeze, aerial hoops, and others. Other circus artists include jugglers, those who practice balancing skills like stilt walkers and unicyclers, contortionists, and puppeteers.

Check out some of the events offered by AYCO to see what it is all about. Every two years, the Biennial National American Youth Circus Festival is held in different places across the United States. Regional festivals provide attendees with the chance to perform and learn new techniques with one-day workshops. They are held every year.

Youth members of the AYCO must pay a small yearly fee to join. Talk to your parents if this is something you are interested in.

Young performers demonstrate just how flexible they are. They can apply their skills not only to aerial silks, but other performing arts as well.

CHAPTER FOUR

STARS OF THE SILKS

The majority of people who learn aerial silks do it for fun or as a good workout. But there is an elite class of athletes who make a living off of their skills. These athletes often come to silks by way of another discipline like dance, gymnastics, acrobatics, or others. While they may be talented athletes, each puts their own spin on their performances.

MAX TORANDELL JOINS THE CIRCUS

A native of Buenos Aires, Argentina, Max Torandell did not start aerial arts until his teenage years. He wanted to be a gymnast or a ballet dancer, but learning circus arts was the next-best thing. Becoming a full-time aerialist never occurred to him, though. In an interview with Jenny of the *Traveling Aerialist* blog, Torandell said: "I was going to school, doing computer science because all of my family was in that business. Then suddenly, I started getting booked for jobs. Then I never stopped; I left computer science on the side and became a performer."

Nicole Winter performs in a dress rehearsal of *iD*, a show by the Canadian circus crew Cirque Eloize at a London show.

Performing and studying in circus schools took Torandell from Argentina to Brazil, Mexico City, and San Francisco, among other places. He worked for Disney South America, Hollywood Aerial Arts, Eyes of New Circus, Cher, Imagination Entertainment, and more. As an aerialist for Cirque du Soleil, he performed for the *Michael Jackson ONE* production in Las Vegas.

His average day while performing in the production started at 3:00 p.m. After two hours putting on make-up, he spent two hours warming up before getting into costume. Next, he performed two shows a night before he left for the day by 11:00 p.m. He repeated this demanding routine five days a week, most of the time while dealing with injuries.

During Torandell's interview with Jenny of the *Traveling Aerialist* blog, he had this to say about his attitude toward his work: "I think what it takes to be the best is not to think of yourself as the best … Even when I have a solo with Cirque du Soleil, if I know someone who is an experienced coach that is in town, I try to get ahold of them for a private training. There is always someone better than you or someone who can help you from a different angle … so I think that is what it takes to be on top of the game. Don't take it for granted and take classes everywhere."

By 2016, Torandell moved into other roles as well as that of aerialist. As of 2019, he worked as a model, choreographer, coach, and artistic director for aerial performances. He makes his home in Los Angeles and travels worldwide for special shows.

A COLORADO SENSATION

Like many aerialists, Denver's Grace Ramsey has a résumé that includes more than one specialty. She performs aerial silks as well as hoops, hammocks, and freestanding hoops. Aerial silks occupied her entirely for six years but these days she has added aerial hoops to her repertoire. In a 2017 interview with the website Vertical Wise, she said: "Aerial is an experience nothing short of spiritual for me. I feel so lucky to be performing and to be good at it. It's a calling."

Ramsey has performed for more than five years on cruise ships, national tours, nightclubs, and festivals. She trains

COSTUMES AND MORE COSTUMES

Other than the silks themselves, one of the most memorable things about aerialists' performances is their costumes. Whether they are snazzy or plain, with sequins or without, there are certain requirements each should have.

First, a costume should protect your body from abrasions or burns from the silks. It is fine—and even encouraged—to have some bare skin, usually on the performer's legs. Costumes should be flattering but not too revealing. The overall look of the costume should be that it is well designed and even expensive. Rhinestones and sequins should be added in order to reflect the light.

In a video interview with journalist Hanna Gelbart for the BBC, aerialist Christine Van Loo said: "What makes a good costume is that, first of all, you feel safe and that you can move well without it falling off. And I like bling, so the more rhinestones the better."

Christine Van Loo makes sure her costumes are free of parts that can snag or tangle.

Costumes for sale can be found on numerous websites such as Etsy, Harmony Threads, Burnt Soul, and others. Or perhaps you would prefer to make your own costume. If you have a talent for sewing, you can start by sewing a basic leotard and adding frills to it. Fabrics high in cotton slip less than those with more Spandex.

about three hours a day four to five days a week. Warm-ups can take two hours. Next, she works on endurance by getting into the air for about twenty-five minutes at a time. After a short break, she does another set. When she is rehearsing for a show, she performs the whole thing until she can do it by memory.

Ramsey downplays the danger of her practice, instead telling future aerialists that the key to safety is to check your rigging and whatever apparatus you are using (such as a hoop or swing) and to be aware of where your body is and what it is doing. She calls this "situational awareness." When asked about the most difficult part of her work, she told Vertical Wise: "Keeping in the right shape." Because Ramsey's work involves projecting a certain image in her performances, she has to be careful to eat right and wear stylish clothes even when off duty.

Ramsey encourages those learning aerial silks to know their limits and keep from comparing themselves to others. After all, the person you are comparing yourself with could have practiced hard to get to where they are. When learners get competitive, it's a guarantee they will eventually hurt themselves.

A SILKEN SKATER

While many aerialists have a background in other athletic practices, Mark Hanretty is unusual. A competitive figure skater, Hanretty decided to add aerial silks to his routine in 2013. When his son was born, he decided he needed to be closer to home. By adding aerial silks to his repertoire, he was able to find work nearer to his home instead of traveling

THE SECRET INGREDIENT IN IMPROVEMENT

Aerialist Christine Van Loo shares some advice about how to achieve professional-level skills with future performers in a video interview with journalist Hanna Gelbart for the BBC: "The thing that helps me the most is not nutrition or supplements or even training. It's 'Am I good enough?' and 'Am I worthy of my dreams?' And when I go through that what I do is I pretend to be the people that I look up to ... when you're emulating somebody, when you're pretending to be someone who you aspire to be, you are improving yourself and becoming as good as that person."

Van Loo swears by this advice, even saying that by modeling her actions on another, more skilled performer, she has become a better athlete—and a better person.

for jobs. Since he is one of the few people to combine both aerial silks and ice-skating, he had to come up with a new name for his act. He went simple, calling it aerial ice.

The most difficult part of combining both disciplines was the sharp ice skate blades cutting his aerial silks and tangling in them. In addition, since performing with aerial silks often requires the performer to climb up the silk, it is extra challenging to climb with the weight of heavy skates.

During his performances, for example, Hanretty grasps silks, one in each hand, and skates in circles with the silks flaring out behind him. He hoists himself up and folds his legs over the top of his head, swinging back and forth as though upside down on a swing. Other times, he wraps the

Mark Hanretty has this to say about talent in an interview with Bill Gibb of the *Sunday Post*: "Hard work is more important than talent."

silks around his ankles and the tops of his skates, doing splits. From there, he climbs up high into the air. He has even hung upside down from silks and grasped hands with another skater, pulling her up into the air!

Hanretty cautions those attempting aerial ice to be very aware of where their blades and silks are in relation to one another. To fail to do this will cause entanglements, slips, and ungainly falls on the ice.

Hanretty lives in the United Kingdom with his family, where they run skate camps for skaters of all ages. In addition to performing aerial ice, he also choreographs routines for figure skaters and ice dancers.

GLOSSARY

aerialist A person who performs acrobatics using silks, hoops, trapeze, or other apparatuses while high above the ground.

array An impressive group.

choreographer A person who arranges dance and movement routines.

contortionist A performer with the ability to twist the body into unlikely positions.

CPR The abbreviation for cardiopulmonary resuscitation, or the procedure to restart a person's breathing process.

credentials Documents that allow a person to perform certain official acts.

empathy The ability to be aware of other people's feelings.

gladiator In ancient Rome, a person who would fight to the death for the entertainment of a crowd.

high-intensity interval training (HIIT) A form of exercise that varies short bursts of intense training with less intense exercises.

invert To turn upside down.

lethal Deadly.

Pilates A form of exercise that makes use of special machines and floor exercises.

repertoire The list of skills possessed by a person.

scaffold A platform built in the air for workers.

trapeze A metal bar that hangs from two ropes at either end.

troupe A company of stage performers.

FOR MORE INFORMATION

Aerial Antics
2215 Gladwin Crescent, Unit 100
Ottawa ON K1B 4K9
Canada
Website: https://www.aerialsottawa.com
Facebook: @aerialanticsottawa
Twitter: @Aerial_Antics
Instagram: @aerialantics
Aerial Antics is a studio that sponsors numerous classes and camps in "mixed aerials" (silks, hoops, hammocks, and trapeze) for kids, teens, and adults.

American Youth Circus Organization (AYCO)
PO Box 482
Ithaca, NY 14851
(914) 441-8834
Website: http://www.americanyouthcircus.org
Facebook: @Americanyouthcircusorganization
Twitter: @IloveAYCO
A national nonprofit organization, the AYCO promotes youth participation in the circus arts.

Circus Arts Institute
2969 East Ponce de Leon Avenue, Suite 370
Decatur, GA 30030
(404) 549-3000
Website: https://www.circusartsinstitute.com
Facebook and YouTube: @circusartsinstitute
Twitter: @circusartsatl
The institute trains the bodies and minds of people interested in the circus arts, from age five through adulthood.

Frequent Flyers Aerial Dance
3022 E. Sterling Circle, #150
Boulder, CO 80301
(303) 245-8272
Website: https://frequentflyers.org
Facebook: @FrequentFlyersAerial
Twitter and Instagram: @freqflyers
This organization puts on the International Aerial Dance Festival in Boulder, Colorado, each summer.

Vancouver Circus School
1525 Welch Street
North Vancouver, BC V7P 1B5
Canada
(604) 544-5024
Website: http://vancouvercircusschool.ca
Facebook, Twitter, and Instagram: @VanCircusSchool
The largest circus school in western Canada, it offers numerous classes in aerial silks for school-aged kids, teens, and adults. A second location has been established in New Westminster, British Columbia.

FOR FURTHER READING

Davis, Jackie Leigh. *DIY Circus Lab for Kids: A Family-Friendly Guide for Juggling, Balancing, Clowning and Show-Making*. Beverly, MA: Quarry Books, 2018.

Delessert, Etienne. *Night Circus*. Mankato, MN: Creative Editions, 2015.

DiPrimio, Pete. *The World of CrossFit*. Hockessin, DE: Mitchell Lane Publishers, 2015.

Luke, Andrew. *Gymnastics*. Broomall, PA: Mason Crest, 2017.

Lusted, Marcia Amidon. *Contortion, German Wheels, and Other Mind-Bending Circus Science.* North Mankato, MN: Capstone Press, 2018.

Lusted, Marcia Amidon. *Trapeze, Perch Poles, and Other High-Flying Circus Science*. North Mankato, MN: Capstone Press, 2018.

Mara, Wil. *Fire Breathing, Sword Swallowing, and Other Death-Defying Circus Science*. North Mankato, MN: Capstone Press, 2018.

McFarland, Emma, and Kate Sutton. *Dance*. Oxford, UK: Oxford University Press 2015.

Rice, Dona. *Circus Fun*. Huntington Beach, CA: Teacher Created Materials, 2018.

Santos, Steven. *Introduction to Rigging: Aerialist Essentials.* Newton, MA: Simply Circus, Inc., 2017.

Wiley, Jack. *Performing Basic Circus Skills*. Scotts Valley, CA: Createspace, 2015.

BIBLIOGRAPHY

Aerial Essentials. Retrieved February 6, 2019. http://aerialessentials.com.

Aerialists.org. "The Beautiful Yet Dangerous Art of Aerial Silk." http://www.aerialists.org/beautiful-dangerous-art-aerial-silk. Retrieved April 19, 2019.

Berzon, Alexandra, and Mark Maremont. "Injuries Put Safety in Spotlight at Cirque Du Soleil." *Wall Street Journal*, April 22, 2015. https://www.wsj.com/articles/injuries-put-safety-in-spotlight-at-cirque-du-soleil-1429723558.

Charley, Lauren. "The Art of Aerial Fitness." *Today Magazine*, September 6, 2018. http://today-magazine.com/art-aeriel-fitness.

Elisara, Rony. "Top Tips to Aerial Success for Beginners!" Aerial Artistry, February 13, 2017. https://www.aerialcircusschool.com/single-post/2016/04/13/Top-Tips-to-Aerial-Success-for-Beginners.

Gelbart, Hannah. "World-Famous Aerialist on the Keys to Her Success." BBC News, July 31, 2018. https://www.bbc.com/news/av/business-44981063/world-famous-aerialist-on-the-keys-to-her-success.

Hanretty, Mark. "Aerialist Skater Promo—Mark Hanretty." YouTube, March 9, 2015. https://youtu.be/t-sOh5u_FxA.

Jenny. "Aerialist Spotlight: Max Torandell's Journey to Cirque Du Soleil." *Traveling Aerialist*, March 9, 2016. https://thetravelingaerialist.wordpress.com/tag/max-torandell.

Karsyn, Ally. "Floating Over an Audience Is Empowering Says Cirque De La Symphonie Aerialist." *Sioux City Journal*, March 14, 2014. https://siouxcityjournal.com/entertainment/arts-and-theatre/floating-over-an-audience-is-empowering-says-cirque-de-la/article_c20ec649-80f5-514a-8fa8-1df312effd21.html.

Kershner, Kate. "10 Circus Safety Strategies the Audience Doesn't See." HowStuffWorks, November 10, 2015. https://entertainment.howstuffworks.com/arts/circus-arts/10-circus-safety-strategies-audience-doesnt-see1.htm.

McInnes, Maren. "BYU's 'Charlotte's Web' Includes Use of Aerial Silks." *Deseret News*, May 22, 2016. https://0-infoweb-newsbank-com.search.tolibrary.org.

100Huntley. "Everything Is Possible / JEN BRICKER." YouTube, November 14, 2016. https://youtu.be/IPuJilt1Tg8.

SEVENTYSINS. "Cirque Du Soleil: Mathieu Lavoie—'Let Me Fall'." YouTube, February 14, 2014. https://www.youtube.com/watch?v=0uCYcN7dRgc.

Thompson, Tony. "Performer Dies in Circus Fall." *Guardian*, August 9, 2003. https://www.theguardian.com/uk/2003/aug/10/tonythompson.theobserver.

Torandell, Max. "Bio." Retrieved February 6, 2019. http://www.maxintheair.com.

Van Loo, Christine. "Performer." Retrieved February 6, 2019. http://www.christinevanloo.com/performer.html.

Vertical Wise. "About Aerial Silks." November 26, 2017. https://www.verticalwise.com/en/about-aerial-silks.

Vertical Wise. "Aerial Ice: A Breathtaking Combination of Ice Skating and Aerial Arts." July 29, 2017. http://www.verticalwise.com/en/mark-hanretty-aerial-ice-skating.

Vertical Wise. "Interview with Aerialist Grace Ramsey." July 12, 2017. http://www.verticalwise.com/en/interview-with-aerialist-grace-ramsey

INDEX

A

acrobat, 7–8, 11–12, 29
acrobatics, 4, 30, 32
aerial dance, 10–11, 16
aerial ice, 37, 39
aerialist
  balance, 6, 19, 22, 28
  beginner, 17–19, 21–23, 27–28
  benefits and challenges of, 4, 6, 17–24, 29, 37
  body strength, 6, 16, 25
  choreography, 23, 34, 39
  coach, 34
  costume, 33–35
  equipment, 6, 10, 12–16, 26–27, 30
  fabric, 12–14, 21, 25, 35
  falls, 15, 17, 25, 27, 30, 35, 39
  fear, 17–18
  flexibility, 16, 19
  injury, 17–19, 21, 25–30, 34
  instructor, 6, 11, 16, 18–22, 27–30
  practice, 16, 18–19, 22–24, 25–26, 29–30, 36
  professional performer, 15, 22–23, 25–28, 32–39
  rigging, 15–16, 27, 36
  risk, 4, 25, 28
  safety, 25, 27, 29–30, 36
  stretching, 14, 16, 19
  technique, 12–16, 17, 22, 31
  training, 6, 18–24, 26–31, 34, 36–37
American Circus Educators, 29–30
American Youth Circus Organization (AYCO), 30–31

B

Bailey, James A., 9–10
Barnum, P. T., 9–10
brain balancing, 28–29

C

camp, 6, 18, 39
certified instructor, 6, 22, 27–31
certified rigger, 15–16
circus, 7–12, 19, 27, 30–31
  aerial performer, 7, 12, 23, 32
  high-wire act, or trapeze, 8–10, 15, 19, 30
  school, 6, 11, 28–30
Cirque de la Symphonie, 11–12, 21, 24
Cirque du Soleil, 4, 6, 10–12, 23, 28, 33–34
contortionist, 4, 12, 30

D

dance
  aerial,10–11, 16
  choreographer, 23, 34, 39
  ice, 37, 39
  studio, 4

E

emergency cut-off switch, 26–27
exercise, 16, 20–21, 28

F

fabric, 12–14, 21, 25, 35
figure skater, 36–37, 39
fitness, 11, 19, 22
foot and leg wrap, 4, 16, 22, 28, 37, 39

G

gym, 4, 28
gymnastics, 19, 21, 29, 32

H

hammock, 15, 21, 34
Hanretty, Mark, 36–37, 39
harness, 10, 25, 27
hoop, or lyra, 15, 30, 34, 36

L

leg and foot wrap, 4, 16, 22, 28, 37, 39

M

mat, 15, 30
music, 4, 8, 11–12, 21, 23–24

R

Ramsey, Grace, 34, 36
Ringling Bros. and Barnum & Bailey Circus, 9–10
rosin, 14

S

scaffold, 15
Sendgraff, Terry, 10
situational awareness, 36
Sky Gym (Atlanta), 28
sling, 15, 21
strap, 15
studio, 4, 6, 11, 18, 28, 30
swing, 9, 15, 22, 25, 36–37

T

therapy, 28
Torandell, Max, 32–34
training, 6, 18–24, 26–31, 34, 36–37
trapeze, or high-wire act, 8–10, 15, 19, 30
Troupe Vertigo, 11

V

Van Loo, Christine, 17, 21, 24, 35, 37

Y

yoga, 4, 19–20

ABOUT THE AUTHOR

Xina M. Uhl vividly remembers watching gymnastics, tumbling, ice-skating, and other acrobatic arts as a child. However, as an adult she writes for educational publications, including books, textbooks, teacher's guides, lessons, and assessment questions. When she is not writing or reading she enjoys travel, photography, and hiking with her dogs. Her blog features her travel adventures and latest fiction projects.

PHOTO CREDITS

Cover, p. 1 Sundraw Photography/Shutterstock.com; p. 5 © AP Images; p. 7 Vladimir Sagadeev/Alamy Stock Photo; pp. 9, 24 Timothy Clary/AFP/Getty Images; p. 10 Album/ Alamy Stock Photo; p. 13 Fancy Studio/Shutterstock.com; p. 14 Vyshedko/Shutterstock.com; pp. 16, 25 Anadolu Agency/ Getty Images; p. 18 4 PM production/Shutterstock.com; p. 21 Maksym Dykha/Shutterstock.com; p. 29 oleg66/E+/Getty Images; p. 31 theatrepix/Alamy Stock Photo; p. 33 Richard Hartog/Los Angeles Times/Getty Images; p. 36 Dave J Hogan/Getty Images; graphic elements chaoss/iStock/Getty Images (gymnast silhouette); RDC_design/iStock/Getty Images (orange grunge background); Vijay Patel/DigitalVision Vectors/Getty Images (black dots background).

Design and Layout: Michael Moy; Photo Researcher: Sherri Jackson